hanging by a thread

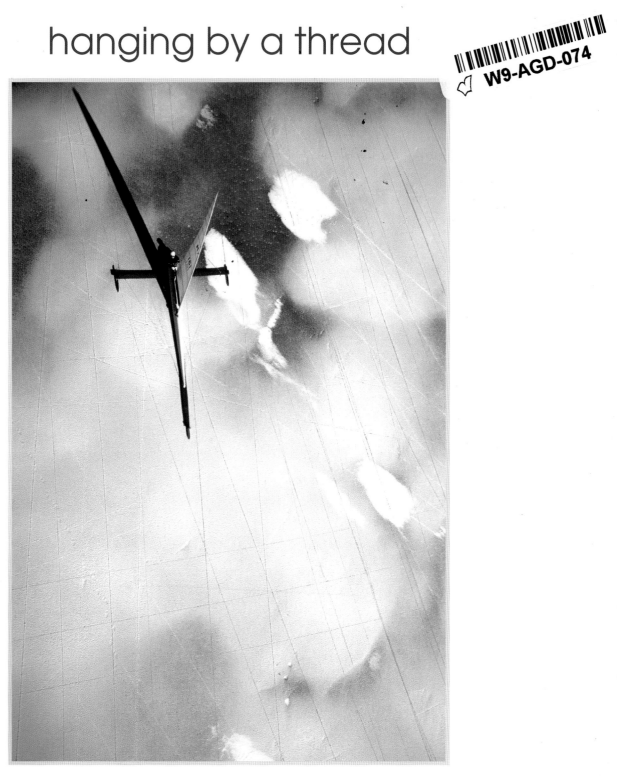

Slippery Sky—Skeeter class iceboat, Lake Mendota   •   *Cielo resbaladizo—trineo de vela clase Skeeter, Lago Mendota*   •

Rutschiger Himmel - Eisboot der Skeeter-Klasse, Mendota-See   •   光滑的天空——门多塔湖上的Skeeter级小型单帆冰上滑艇

(next page) Morning on the Capitol • *(próxima página) Una mañana en el Capitolio* • *(nächste Seite) Morgen am Capitol* •

（次页）州议会大厦的晨曦

hanging by a thread

A KITE'S VIEW OF WISCONSIN

photography by Craig M. Wilson

(above) UW football fans, Breese Terrace, Madison • *(arriba) Fanáticos del fútbol americano de la UW, Terraza Breese, Madison* •
(oben) Football-Fans der Universität Wisconsin, Breese Terrace, Madison • （上）麦迪逊Breese Terrace， 威斯康星大学的橄榄球迷们

Library of Congress Control Number:
2006924044

ISBN 978-0-9761450-3-5

10 9 8 7 6 5 4 3 2 1 *lift off!*

Itchy Cat Press
an Imprint of Flying Fish Graphics
5452 Highway K
Blue Mounds, Wisconsin USA

For Betsy, Madeleine, and Casey

·

In memory of J. Dale

Thanks, Dad, for instilling in me a love of things that fly—
and for the spirit to create things out of what can be found in the garage.

Craig M.Wilson—hanging by a thread
Madison, Wisconsin

Thanks to Scott R. Skinner of the Drachen Foundation,
Seattle, and Todd McGrath of Madison,
for help in funding production of this book,
and for their friendship and support.

Look closely. You'll find Craig in some of the photographs. Follow the thread. • Ponga atención. Encontrará a Craig en algunas de las fotografías. Siga el hilo. • Wenn Sie genau hinsehen, finden Sie Craig in einigen der Fotos. Folgen Sie der Schnur. • 仔细看，你会在一些图片上见到克雷格，跟着线走

Hanging by a Thread: A Kite's View of Wisconsin

Guindando de un Hilo: Viendo a Wisconsin desde un Papagayo

Schweben an der Schnur: Wisconsin aus dem Blickwinkel eines Drachens

标题:《一线相连: 风筝看威州》

foreword

For a medium-sized Midwestern city, Madison has an unusually large community of photographers. This situation might lead to intense competitiveness and a lack of openness and information sharing. Just the opposite is true.

On a regular basis a group of photographers gather to show recent work, discuss new technologies and socialize. It was at one of these gatherings several years ago that I first became aware of Craig Wilson's kite photography.

About a dozen photographers were showing slides and Craig's turn came. The first image I recall him showing was a shot of the gleaming golden statue *Wisconsin* on top of the Wisconsin Capitol dome. Everyone in the room was immediately captivated. The photograph was taken from a vantage point none of us had even imagined before. How had he managed to make a photograph just a few feet away from the statue at a height of over 100 feet? The answer was that Craig had devised an ingenious method of attaching his remote-controlled camera to a kite line.

The group was mesmerized as Craig showed slide after slide using this unusual vantage point, revealing natural and man-made patterns on the ground not otherwise visible.

Everyone who turns the pages of this book will enjoy a unique visual perspective made possible by the dramatic and beautiful kite photography of Craig Wilson.

—*Brent Nicastro*

•

introduction

The thought of using a kite to lift a camera bubbled through my mind. A simple thought, like thousands before it. It seemed possible when I realized my new kite—controlled by my left hand—had more than enough power to lift the camera I held to my eye with my right hand.

That thought struck in 1987, on an afternoon when my big new Delta kite was pulling hard, flying high in the rays of the setting sun. I stood at the end of the line in a meadow, already deep in shadow, wondering what it looks like from up there.

After a few weeks of thinking and tinkering I figured out how I could do it. I needed a timer to epoxy to the back of a camera—a camera that I could live without—a camera I would surely ruin. I waited for the hobby shop to call with the miniature timer I'd ordered, and a few days later emerged from the garage successful. The shutter tripped each time the timer expired. Oh I was proud of myself—so proud of my invention that I wasn't sure I wanted to attach the thing to a kite and risk dashing it to bits. Eventually good judgment gave in to temptation and I gave it a whirl. I sent the camera up the kite line and waited until I thought the timer, rubber bands, and duct tape had tripped the shutter. I retrieved and reset the camera and then repeated it twenty-four more times. It took most of the afternoon.

The next day, I picked up the photos from the lab and saw a roll of poorly framed, blurred pictures that looked like me, or part of me, standing in my backyard. That view from 150 feet up captured on that first roll of film, although technically flawed, ignited a passion in me to figure this thing out. The unique vantage point of a kite-borne camera would allow wonderful, amazing shots. I could see the potential for a system that would actually work. All I needed was a faster camera, better control, more interesting subjects, lots of practice, and lots of film.

Over the next several years, I rebuilt the controllers, bought better cameras, and improved my techniques. I learned to estimate the camera's view because I can't look through the camera when photographing. The kite-borne camera taught me to see pattern, textures, and shapes from above.

So this book is a collection of Wisconsin photos made from a kite. A collection of special treasures, some intended and some unexpected, but treasures discovered along the way.

—Craig M. Wilson
Madison, Wisconsin

(right) Kite's portrait with Craig • *(a la derecha) Retrato del papagayo con Craig* • *(rechts) Craig mit dem Drachen* • （右）风筝和克雷格的肖像

The Shadow knows . . . • *La sombra sabe . . .* • *Der Schatten verrät es . . .* • 阴影知晓……

Fun on the carnival rides at a Monona festival • *Paseos en el parque de diversiones, en un festival en Monona* • *Spaß auf den Rides bei einem Fest in Monona* • 在莫诺纳节日上狂欢骑乘趣事

John Nolen Drive along Lake Monona with Lake Mendota in background, Madison • John Nolen Drive a lo largo de Lago Monona con el Lago Mendota al fondo, Madison • Die John Nolen Drive entlang des Monona-Sees mit dem Mendota-See im Hintergrund, Madison • 麦迪逊沿莫诺纳湖的约翰•诺伦大道，背景是门多塔湖

"Wisconsin" on the Capitol dome looking over Lake Monona • *"Wisconsin" en el domo del Capitolio, contemplando a Lago Monona* •
„Wisconsin" auf dem Dom des Capitols blickt über den Monona-See • 透过州议会大厦拱顶俯瞰莫诺纳湖所见之"威斯康星"

Governor's residence on Lake Mendota • *Residencia del Gobernador en el Lago Mendota* • *Gouverneursresidenz am Mendota-See* •
门多塔湖上的州长府邸

(pages 6–7) Concert on the Square—Wisconsin Chamber Orchestra on the Capitol lawn • *(páginas 6–7) Concierto en la Cuadra —Orquesta de Cámara de Wisconsin en la grama del Capitolio* • *(Seite 6–7) Platzkonzert - Kammerorchester von Wisconsin auf dem Rasen des Capitols* • （第6至7页）广场上的音乐会 —— 威斯康星室内乐乐团在州议会大厦草坪上演奏

(left) Music lovers, Concert on the Square • *(a la izquierda) Amantes de la música, Concierto en la Cuadra* • *(links) Musikliebhaber, Platzkonzert* • （左）欣赏广场音乐会的音乐爱好者们

(above) Concert in the Park, Middleton • *(arriba) Concierto en el Parque, Middleton* • *(oben) Konzert im Park, Middleton* • （上部）在米德尔顿的公园中举办的音乐会

(left) Frank Lloyd Wright's Monona Terrace, Madison • *(a la izquierda) Terraza Monona de Frank Lloyd Wright, Madison* •
(links) Die Monona-Terrasse von Frank Lloyd Wright, Madison • （左）弗朗克•劳埃德•赖特设计的麦迪逊莫诺纳露台

(above) Friendly chat • *(arriba) Conversación amigable* • *(oben) Freundliches Schwätzchen* • （上）友好闲聊

Otis Redding Memorial • *Monumento Otis Redding* • *Otis Redding-Denkmal* • 奥蒂斯•雷丁纪念园

Brat Fest, Madison • *Festival de Salchichas, Madison* • *Brat Fest, Madison* • 麦迪逊的布拉特节

almost busted

Good lighting alone won't do it. I need wind of the right speed and direction to photograph the Capitol. Forget scheduling a time—when the conditions are right I have to get there fast.

I found a perfect time one late Sunday afternoon and quickly had my camera up over the Capitol shooting in exceptional light and wind. I was hoping for a golden sunset on the Capitol. Out of the corner of my eye, I noticed a flashing light and looked over to see a police car screeching to a halt.

An officer hurled himself out the door and ran towards me. His hand was on his holstered weapon and he yelled at me, "Bring that kite down immediately. If you don't, I'll do it for you!"

I looked at him, smiled, and said calmly, "Sir, you seem a bit upset. What is the problem? It is just a kite with a camera." He yelled at me, "You have three seconds to get that down!" I said "Sir, it will take me longer than that to get it down. It's not safe to land it here."

I explained that a camera hung from the line, I was simply taking pictures, and asked why he was so worried. He said I might be "trying to deliver something into the air ducts of the building." I hoped he didn't see my eyes roll. As we talked he calmed down. He could see I knew how to handle the sizable kite, that it had considerable pull, and if he was going to bring it down forcibly, he was going to have his hands full.

He continued to insist that I bring the kite down so that he could confirm that the object attached to the line was indeed a camera. I explained we had to walk the airborne kite to the rooftop park two blocks away where I launched it. I could land it safely there.

I offered to wait for him while he moved his car, which was still in the middle of the road with the door open and the engine running. He thought for a moment and then radioed his backup and told him to take care of the car—he was busy with "the suspect."

I said, "So you don't trust me. Sir, I can't run off with a 20-foot kite in the air. Really, I'll wait for you."

"No," he said, "I am staying with you."

So we started to walk down Martin Luther King Jr. Blvd. to the rooftop park of Monona Terrace. We talked along the way and he, a bit calmer now, said he appreciated my cooperation and began asking questions about how this thing worked. He watched the camera swing while I demonstrated the controls. I took a nice shot of the Capitol, and we continued onto the rooftop chatting about the kite and the radio controls for the camera. I anchored the kite to a railing and brought the camera down to ground level. Officer Calhoun confirmed that indeed it was a camera and we posed for a photo shaking hands.

He told me that I needed a permit to fly over the Capitol. I said okay and I asked him to turn and look at the pink light on the Capitol.

"That," I said, "is what I had been trying to catch." The next day I filed for a permit.

(left and above) Capitol at sunset • *(a la izquierda y arriba) La puesta del sol en el Capitolio* •
(links und oben) Capitol bei Sonnenuntergang •
（左部与上部）夕阳下的州议会大厦

(right) Officer Calhoun and me • *(a la derecha) Oficial Calhoun y yo* • *(rechts) Polizeibeamter Calhoun und ich* •
（右）卡尔霍恩警官与我合影

(pages 16–17) Union Worker, Memorial Union Terrace, UW-Madison • *(páginas 16–17) Estudiando duro, Terraza Memorial Union, UW-Madison* • *(Seite 16–17) Arbeitender Student, Memorial Union-Terrasse, UW-Madison* •
（第16至17页）麦迪逊威斯康星大学的纪念协会露台和协会工作者

(left) 470 sailboats, Memorial Union • *(a la izquierda) 470 veleros, Memorial Union* • *(links) 470 Segelboote, Memorial Union* •
（左）纪念协会，470条帆船

(above) Paddle and Portage start, James Madison Park • *(arriba) Partida de Paddle and Portage, Parque James Madison* •
(oben) Start des „Paddle and Portage"-Rennens, James Madison Park • （上）詹姆斯·麦迪逊公园的水陆联运始发点

(above) Shells on shore, Lake Monona • (arriba) "Conchas en la playa", Lago Monona • (oben) Muscheln am Ufer, Monona-See • （上）莫多纳湖畔的赛艇

(right) Canoes at rest • (a la derecha) Canoas descansando • (rechts) Ruhende Kanus • （右）停靠着的独木舟

(left) Capitol and State Street • *(a la izquierda) Capitolio y State Street* • *(links) Capitol und State Street* •
（左）州议会大厦与斯泰特大街

(above) Wishing, Library Mall, UW-Madison • *(arriba) La "fuente de los deseos", Library Mall, UW-Madison* • *(oben) Wünsch
dir was, Library Mall, Universität Wisconsin, Madison* • （上）麦迪逊-威斯康星大学图书馆商场，愿望

Thai Pavilion, Olbrich Botanical Gardens   •   Pabellón Thai, Jardines Botánicos Olbrich   •   Thailändischer Pavillon, Botanische Gärten von Olbrich   •   奥尔布里奇（Olbrich）植物园的泰国式亭子

Olbrich Fountain • *Fuente Olbrich* • *Olbrich-Brunnen* • 奥尔布里奇喷泉

wishing

I was lucky; I could spend so much time taking photographs because I excused trips to the park with the kids and my kite as "good parenting."

"Hon, you get some sleep, I'm going to the park with the kids."

Then at the park, "Okay, kids, how 'bout you go play on the swings."

"How 'bout you climb on those monkey bars."

"How 'bout you throw the ball with your sister."

"How 'bout you carry this kite line and these kites."

"How 'bout you two stand by the fountain. Now hold still and make like you're wishing for something."

I think I know what they wished for.

It didn't take long for them to figure it out. When I would ask if they wanted to go to the park, they would reply, "Are you going to take kites?"

(left) Rhapsody in Bloom Party in the garden • *(a la izquierda) Fiesta "Rapsodia Floreciente" en el jardín* • *(links) „Blühende Rapsodie"-Party im Garten* • （左）植物园中花季聚会

(above) Picnic in clover • *(arriba) ¡Picnic a lo grande!* • *(oben) Picknick im Klee* • （上）在苜蓿从中野餐

Art Fair Off the Square, Madison • *Feria de Arte fuera de la Cuadra, Madison* • *Kunstmesse, Madison* •
麦迪逊，广场旁边的艺术品交易会

Bridge fishing, Brittingham Bay, Lake Monona • *Pescando desde el puente, Bahía Brittingham, Lago Monona* • *Angeln von der Brücke, Brittingham Bay, Monona-See* • 桥上垂钓，莫诺纳湖布里丁汉湾

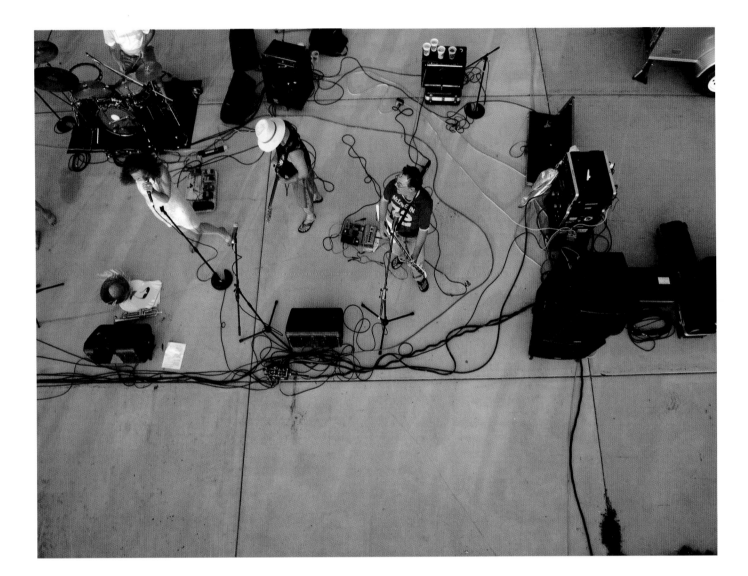

(above) Reptile Palace Orchestra • *(arriba) Orquesta Palacio de Reptiles* • *(oben) Das Reptile Palace Orchestra* •
（上）雷普泰尔派雷斯（Reptile Palace）交响乐团

(right) Hanging by a Thread at the Blues Festival • *(a la derecha) Guindando de un hilo en el Festival de Blues* •
(rechts) Auf dem Blues-Festival an der Schnur hängend • （右）在布鲁斯音乐节上用线吊挂起来

(left) Blues Fest • *(a la izquierda) Festival de Blues* • *(links) Blues-Fest* • （左）布鲁斯音乐节

(above) Opera in the Park, Madison • *(arriba) Ópera en el Parque, Madison* • *(oben) Oper im Park, Madison* •
（上）麦迪逊，公园中演唱的歌剧

leave it to maddy

It was one of those beautiful October afternoons with little white puffy clouds floating across the sky and fall colors in full glory. That crisp, brilliant kind of day that you get only a couple times each year here in Wisconsin.

I asked Madeleine if she would help me make a photo out in the front yard. The trees were golden, the sun angle and the wind were just right, and the yard needed raking. Perfect!

After some negotiation she agreed to pose with the rake, but not actually *do* any raking. I couldn't argue; I would be flying a kite.

I headed up to the open greenway at the end of the cul-de-sac to launch the kite and camera and then maneuver it back to our yard. Madeleine put on a sweatshirt, found the rake, and waited for me in the front yard.

The cool breeze was steady, allowing the camera to float at treetop level. I positioned the camera to capture the treetops, still holding their golden leaves, and Madeleine below with her rake. I walked back and forth moving the camera between the trees. Madeleine didn't say much; she just seemed to be putzing around with the rake. I shot a dozen images and decided we had done all we could.

Next day I looked at the slides on the light table and burst out laughing as I discovered that Madeleine had raked a happy face of leaves. I had walked across it several times without noticing the pattern she had created. It was the kite's view that revealed her subtle, clever humor.

(right) Recycle—Fall Colorfest race, La Grange, Walworth County • (a la derecha) Carrera de bicicletas "Festival de los Colores de Otoño", La Grange, Condado de Walworth • (rechts) Recycle - Colorfest-Rennen im Herbst, La Grange, Walworth County •

（右）再循环——沃尔华斯县拉格朗日（La Grange）秋色盛会比赛

(left top) Neighborhood colors • *(arriba a la izquierda) Colores del vecindario* • *(links oben) Farben eines Stadtviertels* •
（左上）邻里色彩斑斓

(left bottom) Bus load • *(abajo a la izquierda) Montándose en el autobús* • *(links unten) Busbeladung* • （左下）乘公共汽车

(above) Rock climb • *(arriba) Escalando una roca* • *(oben) Felsenklettern* • （上）攀岩

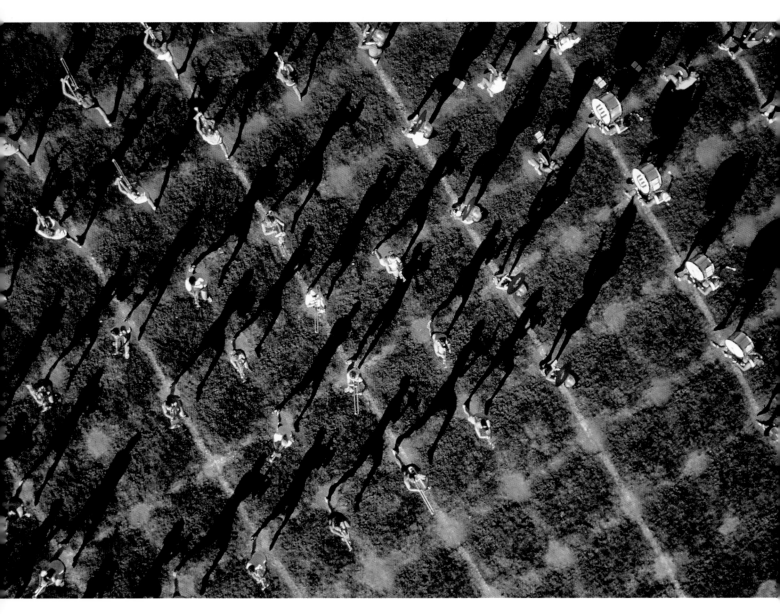

kokopellis

I took the long way home through the UW campus from downtown looking for an interesting photo opportunity. I found the UW marching band practicing with the late sunlight creating long, hard shadows. I quickly got my big Delta kite assembled and into the air, then worked my camera around the band, dodging their high steps, quick turns, and about-faces.

(above) UW Alumni band marches into Camp Randall • *(arriba) Banda de alumnos egresados de la UW, marchando hacia el Campo Randall* • *(oben) Studentenband der Universität Wisconsin marschiert ins Camp Randall-Stadium* • （上）威斯康星大学校友会乐队开进兰德尔营地

(pages 40–41) Badger Game Day, UW football • *(páginas 40–41) Juego de los Badger, equipo de fútbol de la UW* • *(Seite 40–41) Football-Spieltag der Badgers, Universität Wisconsin* • （第40至41页）威斯康星大学橄榄球獾队比赛日

(left) Head game, Camp Randall student section • *(a la izquierda) "Juego de cabezas", sección de estudiantes del Campo Randall* •
(links) Viele Köpfe im Studentenabschnitt des Camp Randall-Stadiums • （左）观看比赛的人群，兰德尔营地的学生

(above) Madison Dog Jog for the Humane Society • *(arriba) Caminata con Perros en Madison para beneficio de la
Sociedad Humana* • *(oben) Madison Hundejoggen für den Tierschutzverein* • （上）为慈善协会举办的麦迪逊跑狗赛

(above) Sailboats at Memorial Union pier • (arriba) Veleros en el muelle Memorial Union • (oben) Segelboote am Memorial Union-Pier • （上）"纪念协会"码头上的帆船

(right) Party time on the terrace • (a la derecha) Hora de divertirse en la terraza • (rechts) Partyzeit auf der Terasse • （右）露台上的聚会

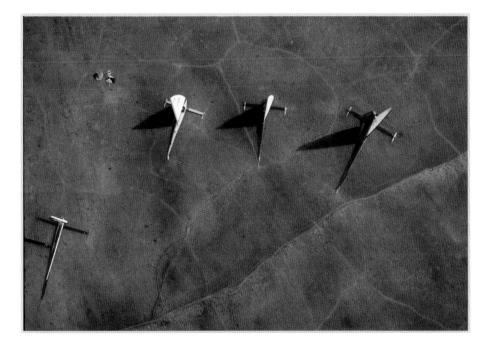

fast friends

A friend invited me to come out on frozen Lake Mendota to watch him race his iceboat. I guessed that iceboats might be good subjects but I hesitated, thinking I would be in the way and standing close to boats traveling 60 to 100 miles per hour could be dangerous. I decided to take him up on the offer.

I parked my car, put on my hockey skates, and then began towing a sled with my gear, out towards the collection of triangular sails. After twenty minutes of skating, I arrived at the downwind mark of the racecourse, changed to boots and crampons, and set up my kite.

The kite rose quickly in the clear smooth air and in no time I had a camera airborne. I walked around the boats making photos but getting glares from some of the sailors. I heard comments: "Hey, what's that guy with the kite doing, we're trying to have a race here." I did some explaining but I felt only a few people understood what I was doing. I shot some rolls of film and left, hoping that I had some decent photos.

The next day, I was stunned by the new images on my light table. The boats looked good but it was the ice that really blew me away. The aerial view revealed so much more than the view from the surface. I knew right away that I'd go back for more shots the next time they raced. To my surprise, I got an e-mail from the commodore of the club asking if my photos had turned out. I said, "They sure did," and that I wanted to come back again to shoot some more. He said, "Sure," and asked if I would be interested in giving a slide show at the next club meeting.

The next weekend, I was back at the race site, and moved around with more confidence. I took photos of the parked boats and their crews, and maneuvered into position to photograph the boats while they were racing. Some of the sailors greeted me and posed with their boats. They asked about the shots from the week before and I noticed some of them studying my kite to judge the wind, trying to gain an edge in the next race.

Again when I got the film back from the lab I was astounded at the way the ice looked. Wednesday night at the meeting the room grew quiet and jaws dropped when I projected my images on the screen. Iceboaters spend every weekend daylight hour on frozen lakes when conditions are right. They often travel great distances to find good ice. These sailors know the lakes and they really know ice, but they had never seen ice from this perspective. They couldn't believe what they were seeing.

I didn't make the next race but I heard that people asked, "Hey, where is the kite guy?"

(left) Icicle Built for Two • *(a la izquierda) Carámbano de hielo justo para dos* • *(links) In trauter Eintracht* •
（左）为两人生成的冰柱

(above) Late season ice • *(arriba) Hielo a finales de la estación de invierno* • *(oben) Eis der späten Saison* • （上）迟迟未解冻的冰

(left) Iceboats on Lake Mendota • *(a la izquierda) Trineos de vela en el Lago Mendota* • *(links) Eisboote auf dem Mendota-See* •
（左）门多塔湖上的冰上滑艇

(above) Lake Geneva iceboats set up • *(arriba) Preparando los trineos de vela en el Lago Geneva* • *(oben) Aufbau der Eisboote auf dem Geneva-See* • （上）日内瓦湖冰上滑艇准备起航

(above) Renegade class iceboats passing the upwind mark • *(arriba) Trineos de vela de la clase Renegade, pasando la marca en contra del viento* • *(oben) Eisboote der Renegade-Klasse passieren die luvseitige Wendemarke* • （上）"叛逆者"级冰上滑艇驶过逆风标

(right top) Cross country skiing • *(arriba a la derecha) Esquiando* • *(rechts oben) Skilaufen in der Umgebung* • （右上）乡间滑雪

(right bottom) Skating at Vilas Park, Madison • *(abajo a la derecha) Patinando sobre hielo en Parque Vilas, Madison* • *(rechts unten) Eislaufen bei Vilas Park, Madison* • （右下）在麦迪逊维拉斯公园（Vilas Park）溜冰

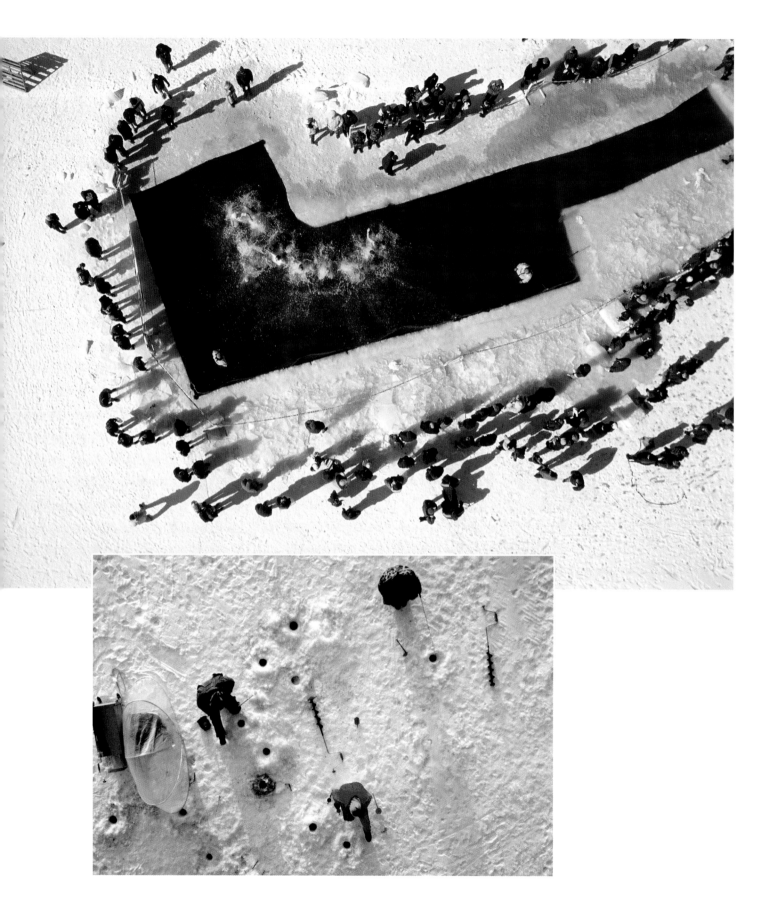

(left top) Shrinkage—Polar Plunge in Lake Wingra, Vilas Park • *(arriba a la izquierda) ¡Desafiando el frío!—Lanzándose en el Lago Wingra, Parque Vilas* • *(links oben) Schrumpelig vor Kälte - Eiskaltes Eintauchen in den Wingra-See, Vilas Park* • （左上）收缩——在维拉斯公园温格拉湖冬泳

(left bottom) Ice fishing • *(abajo a la izquierda) Pescando en el hielo* • *(links unten) Eisfischen* • （左下）冰上捕鱼

(above) Sleigh rides • *(arriba) Paseos en trineo* • *(oben) Schlittenfahrten* • （上）乘雪橇

(pages 54–55) Bert and Ernie, Kites on Ice, Madison   •   *(páginas 54–55) Bert y Ernie, espectáculo Papagayos sobre Hielo, Madison*   •

(Seite 54–55) Bert und Ernie, Veranstaltung „Drachen auf dem Eis", Madison   •   （第54至55页）伯特与厄尼，麦迪逊的冰上风筝

(above) Top of the hill   •   *(arriba) La cima de la colina*   •   *(oben) Auf der Spitze des Hügels*   •   （上）山顶

Kites on Ice, Lake Monona •
Espectáculo Papagayos sobre Hielo,
Lago Monona • *Veranstaltung*
„Drachen auf dem Eis", Monona-See •
在莫诺纳湖的冰上放风筝

Welcome to Madison — David Medaris shovels a greeting • *Bienvenidos a Madison — David Medaris dando la bienvenida con una pala y la nieve* • *Willkommen in Madison - David Medaris schaufelt eine Begrüßung* • 欢迎来到麦迪逊——戴维•梅达里斯铲出的问候语

Hockey tree • *"Un árbol de hockey sobre hielo"* • *Hockey-Baum* • 冰上曲棍球树

Winter storage • *"Almacén del invierno"* • *Winterlagerung* • 冬季库房

(above) Balloon rally, Wisconsin Dells • *(arriba) Carrera de globos de aire, Wisconsin Dells* • *(oben) Heißluftballon-Veranstaltung, Wisconsin Dells* • （上）威斯康星幽谷放气球大会

(right) Burt Rutan's White Knight rocket plane atop Spaceship One • *(a la derecha) Aeroplano White Knight de Burt Rutan, encima del Spaceship One* • *(rechts) Burt Rutans Raketenflugzeug „White Knight" oben auf dem „Spaceship One"* • （右）伯特·拉坦的"白骑士"火箭式推进飞机在飞船一号顶上

experimentation

Airplanes were always under construction in the garage when I was growing up. I had a small hand in those projects; I held the "dumb end" of the tape measure, caught Sitka spruce as it came out of the table saw, and stitched fabric to wings. I earned lots of plane rides and annual pilgrimages to the Mecca of sport aviation—Oshkosh, Wisconsin.

I was honored when the Experimental Aircraft Association asked to exhibit a collection of my kite aerial photos in the AirVenture Museum. During that show, I approached the museum director about flying a kite and making photos at the EAA convention. I was somewhat surprised when he said he thought it was a good idea and would see what he could do to make it happen.

So, I found myself flying my home-built kite, dangling a camera over priceless airplanes at the heart of the largest aircraft gathering in the world. Adam, the museum director—my chaperone—talked constantly on the phone to the control tower, flight operations, airport security, and EAA officials. He choreographed a dance for my twenty-foot kite in an airspace crowded with commercial traffic, air-show flights, ultralights, and helicopters.

When I finished the shoot and landed my kite and camera safely back on the ground, I was thankful but amazed that EAA allowed me to fly a kite up in that airspace. There was still room in this world for adventure and innovation. Then it struck me; the EAA is all about experimentation and adventure—it says so right in its name— and much of that experimentation started out in people's garages. These are my kind of people.

Aero Shell Square, center stage at EAA Fly-In, Oshkosh • *Aero Shell Square, en primer plano en el EAA Fly-In, Oshkosh* •

Aero Shell Square, Mittelpunkt der Flugshow EAA Fly-In, Oshkosh • 奥什科什的飞机广场上EAA Fly-In的中央一景

EAA Homebuilt parking areas • Áreas de estacionamiento EAA Homebuilt • Parkbereiche für EAA-Selbstbauflugzeug •
EAA的停机坪

EAA Homebuilt camping section   •   Secciones para acampar EAA Homebuilt   •   Campingbereich für EAA-Selbstbauflugzeuge   •
EAA的营地

(above) Autumn colors, Cazenovia • *(arriba) Colores de otoño, Cazenovia* • *(oben) Herbstfarben, Cazenovia* • （上）卡扎诺维亚的秋色

(right) Holy cow! • *(a la derecha) ¡Alguien me está viendo!* • *(rechts) Da staunen die Kühe!* • （右）圣牛！

(left top) Farming contours, Belleville • *(arriba a la izquierda) "Granjas curveadas", Belleville* • *(links oben) Feldkonturen, Belleville* • （左上）贝拉维尔农耕风貌

(left bottom) Windmill, Sauk County • *(abajo a la izquierda) Molino de viento, Condado de Sauk* • *(links unten) Windmühle, Sauk County* • （左下）索克县的风车

(above) Ready for picking • *(arriba) Listos para recoger* • *(oben) Erntereif* • （上）只待收获

Schuster Farm, fall harvest, Deerfield • *Granja Schuster, cosecha del otoño, Deerfield* • *Schuster Farm, Herbsternte, Deerfield* •
迪尔菲尔德，秋收时节的舒斯特农场

Stockade, Aztalan State Park •
Aztalan州立公园

Pumpkin pick, Iowa County • *Recogiendo calabazas, Condado de Iowa* • *Kürbiswahl, Iowa County* • 爱荷华县，收南瓜

(left top) Whooping Cranes—the work of crop artist Stan Herd, Newburg • *(arriba a la izquierda) Grullas ruidosas—la obra del artista de la cosecha Stan Herd, Newburg* • *(links oben) Schreikraniche - die Arbeit des Feldkünstlers Stan Herd, Newburg* •（左上）欢鸣的仙鹤——纽堡一位农作物艺术家的作品

(left bottom) Aldo Leopold Nature Center, Monona • *(abajo a la izquierda) Centro Natural Aldo Leopold, Monona* • *(links unten) Naturzentrum Aldo Leopold, Monona* •（左下）莫诺纳，阿尔多•列奥波德自然保护中心

(above) Laux Cranberry Bogs, Harshaw, Oneida County • *(arriba) Laux Cranberry Bogs, Harshaw, Condado de Oneida* • *(oben) Laux Cranberry-Sumpfbeete, Harshaw, Oneida County* •（上）奥涅达县哈斯少的Laux 越菊种植场

(left top) Hauge Log Church, Dane County • (arriba a la izquierda) Iglesia de Trozos de Madera Hauge, Condado de Dane •
(links oben) Hauge Log-Kirche, Dane County • （左上）达讷县豪格劳格（Hauge Log）教堂

(left bottom) Dickeyville Grotto • (abajo a la izquierda) Dickeyville Grotto • (links unten) Dickeyville Grotto •
（左下）迪基维尔（Dickeyville）洞穴

(above) Long-term parking, Dickeyville Grotto Cemetery • (arriba) "Estacionamiento a largo plazo", Cementerio Dickeyville Grotto •
(oben) Langzeitparkplatz, Friedhof von Dickeyville Grotto • （上）迪基维尔洞穴公墓的长期停车场

The High Ground, Viet Nam War Veterans Memorial, Neillsville • *The High Ground, Monumento a los Veteranos de la Guerra de Vietnam, Neillsville* • *„The High Ground", Denkmal für Vietnam-Kriegsveteranen, Neillsville* •

尼尔斯维尔越南战争退伍军人纪念碑的高地

Morning fog at Villa Louis State Park, Mississippi River • *Neblina en la mañana, en el Parque Estatal Villa Louis, Río Mississippi* •
Morgennebel im Villa Louis State Park am Mississippi-Fluss • 密西西比河畔维拉•路易州立公园的晨雾

Villa Louis on the Mississippi River • *Villa Louis en el Río Mississippi* • *Villa Louis am Mississippi-Fluss* •
密西西比河畔维拉 • 路易

Beans and corn—loading barges on the Mississippi River • Granos y maíz—cargando barcazas en el Río Mississippi •
Bohnen und Mais - Beladen von Lastkähnen am Mississippi-Fluss • 豆子和玉米 —— 密西西比河满载的卡车和驳船

(above) University of Wisconsin-Whitewater band • *(arriba) Universidad de Wisconsin-banda de Whitewater* •

(oben) Band der Universität Wisconsin-Whitewater • （上）威斯康星大学——怀特沃特乐队

(right) Home game, UW-Whitewater • *(a la derecha) Juego deportivo, UW-Whitewater* • *(rechts) Heimspiel, UW-Whitewater* •

（右）威斯康星大学怀特沃特乐队在主场

(left) Go, Warhawks! • *(a la izquierda) ¡Arriba, Warhawks!* • *(links) Warhawks vor!* • （左）加油，战鹰！

(above) UW-Whitewater women's soccer team • *(arriba) Equipo femenino de balompié de la UW-Whitewater* •
(oben) Frauenfußballmannschaft der Universität Wisconsin-Whitewater • （上）威斯康星大学怀特沃特女子足球队

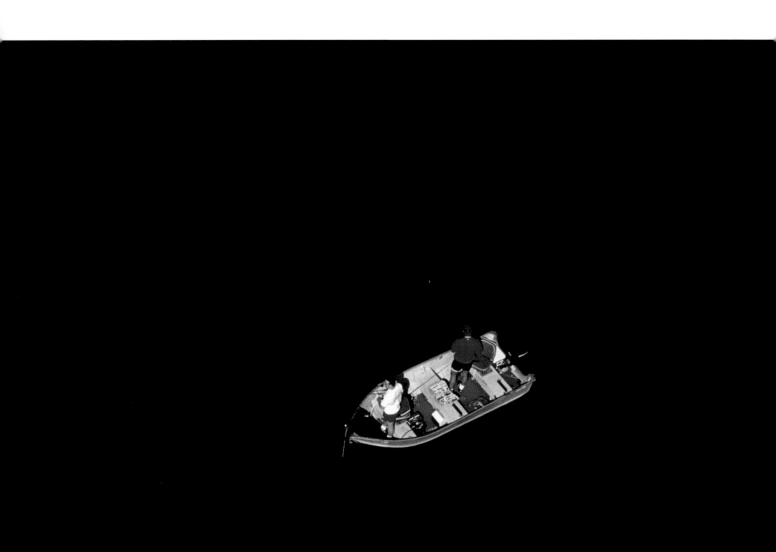

Gone fishing • *Yendo de pesca* • *Angler* • 去捕鱼

Say ahhhh—Freshwater Fishing Hall of Fame, Hayward • *Diga ¡ahhhh!—Sala de Fama para la Pesca en Agua Dulce, Hayward* •
Bitte den Mund weit aufmachen - „Hall of Fame" für Frischwasserangeln, Hayward • 啊！——海沃德"清水钓鱼鱼嘴大厅"

Kayakers on Lake Columbia, Portage power plant • "Kayakers" en el Lago Columbia, planta eléctrica de Portage • Kayaker auf dem Columbia-See, Kraftwerk Portage • 波蒂奇（Portage）发电厂，哥伦比亚湖上的皮艇

Mississippi River fishing   •   *Pescando en el Río Mississippi*   •   *Angeln am Mississippi-Fluss*   •   在密西西比河上捕鱼

not a shore thing

Flying a large kite with electronics and a camera attached takes concentration. Add a boat and you really have your hands full. So early on, I drafted my son, Casey, for the boat driver job. On open water, there are no power lines or trees to snag the kite. The wind is usually steady and if it's not blowing, the forward motion of the boat creates lift for the kite. There are new and interesting photos to be taken from boats—as long as I keep the camera out of the water.

Casey drives, and I handle the kite. We've had good times boating and kiting in sailboat races, among canoes, fishermen, and party boats. The best was the day on the Willow Flowage in northern Wisconsin when three young golden eagles flew around the airborne kite.

Paul Fieber

(above) Tech dinghies on Lake Mendota • *(arriba) Botes en el Lago Mendota* • *(oben) Tech-Dingis auf dem Mendota-See* •
（上）门多塔湖上的技术级小舢板

(right) Kite launch • *(a la derecha) Lanzando el papagayo* •
(rechts) Start eines Drachen • （右）风筝起飞了

(next page) Gilligan's Island, Yahara River • *(próxima página) La Isla de Gilligan, Río Yahara* •
(nächste Seite) Gilligan-Insel, Yahara-Fluss • （次页）亚哈拉河上的吉利甘岛屿

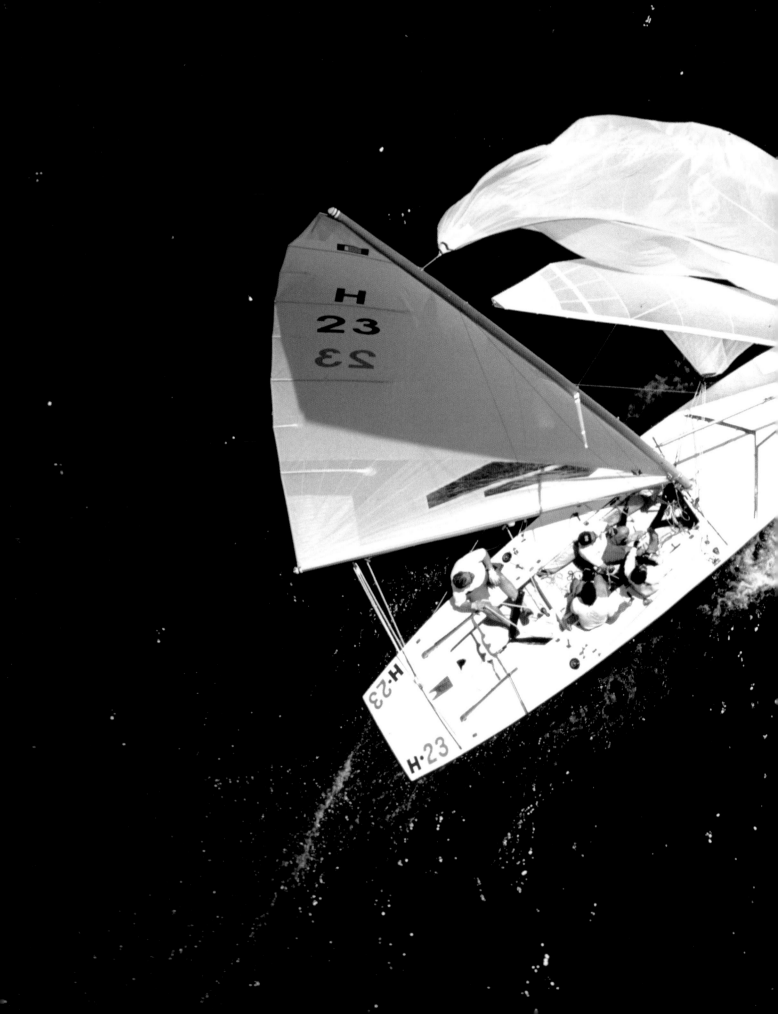

(pages 88–89) Celestial Navigator, E-boat on Lake Mendota • *(páginas 88–89) "Navegante Celestial", E-boat en el Lago Mendota* • *(Seite 88–89) Astronavigator, Boot der E-Klasse auf dem Mendota-See* •

（第88至89页）门多塔湖上的电动船 "天上航行者" 号

(above) Bay Fest Sand Man, Green Bay • *(arriba) Hombre de Arena del Festival de la Bahía Bay, Green Bay* •
(oben) Mann aus Sand auf dem Bay Fest, Green Bay • （上）格林湾，湾区集会上的沙人

Windsurfing lesson, Lake Michigan • *Lección de winsurfing, Lago Michigan* • *Windsurfing-Unterricht, Michigan-See* •
密歇根湖上的帆板运动课

Sheboygan lighthouse • *Faro de Sheboygan* • *Sheboygan-Leuchtturm* • 谢博伊甘（Sheboygan）灯塔

Racine Harbor • *Puerto de Racine* • *Racine-Hafen* • 拉西内（Racine）港

(left top) Highway 42, Ephraim, Door County • *(arriba a la izquierda) Autopista 42, Ephraim, Condado de Door* •
(links oben) Highway 42, Ephraim, Door County • （左上）多尔县，埃弗雷姆（Ephraim），第42号公路

(left bottom) Eagle Harbor, Ephraim • *(abajo a la izquierda) Puerto Eagle, Ephraim* • *(links unten) Eagle-Hafen, Ephraim* •
（左下）埃弗雷姆，鹰港

(above) Cana Island Light, 3rd order Fresnel lens • *(arriba) Faro de la Isla Cana, lentes Fresnel de 3ra orden* • *(oben) Cana Island-Leuchtfeuer, Fresnel-Linse dritter Ordnung* • （上）用第三级透镜摄取的卡纳岛（Cana Island）上的灯塔

Cana Island lighthouse, Lake Michigan, built 1869 • *Faro de la Isla Cana, Lago Michigan, construido en 1869* •

Cana Island-Leuchtturm, Michigan-See, 1869 gebaut • 建造于1869年的密歇根湖畔卡纳岛灯塔

Rock On! Washington Island •
¡Rock On! Isla de Washington •
Washington Island ist Spitze! •
华盛顿岛上的石头

Potawatomi State Park tower, Door County • *Torre del Parque Estatal Potawatomi, Condado de Door* • *Turm im Potawatomi State Park, Door County* • Potawatomi州立公园塔，多尔县

Old Sturgeon Bay bridge, Door Peninsula • *Puente en la Old Sturgeon Bay, Península de Door* • *Old Sturgeon Bay-Brücke, Halbinsel „Door Peninsula"* • 多尔半岛上古老的斯特金港湾桥

Maritime Museum Harbor, Sturgeon Bay • *Puerto del Museo Marítimo, Bahía Sturgeon* • *Maritimmuseum Harbor, Sturgeon Bay* • 斯特金港湾海事博物馆港口

Frank Lloyd Wright Visitor Center, Wisconsin River • *Centro de Visitantes Frank Lloyd Wright, Río Wisconsin* • *Frank Lloyd Wright-Besucherzentrum, Wisconsin-Fluss* • 威斯康星河，弗朗克•劳埃德•赖特访问者中心

Crystal Lake Campground, Columbia County • *Campamento del Lago Crystal, Condado de Columbia* • *Campingplatz "Crystal Lake", Columbia County* • 哥伦比亚县，克里斯特尔湖畔

Mirror Lake, autumn colors • *Lago Mirror, colores de otoño* • *Mirror Lake - der Spiegelsee in Herbstfarben* • 镜湖秋色

Tiffany Bridge, Turtle Creek, Rock County. The only five-arch masonry railway bridge in the country, built 1869 • *Puente Tiffany, Arroyuelo Turtle, Condado de Rock. El único puente ferroviario de cinco arcos y hecho de mampostería que existe en el país, construido en 1869* • *Tiffany-Brücke, Turtle Creek, Rock County Die einzige fünfbogige Eisenbahnsteinbrücke im Land, 1869 gebaut* •

洛克县，龟溪蒂凡尼桥，建造于1869年的该县唯一一座五孔公路石桥

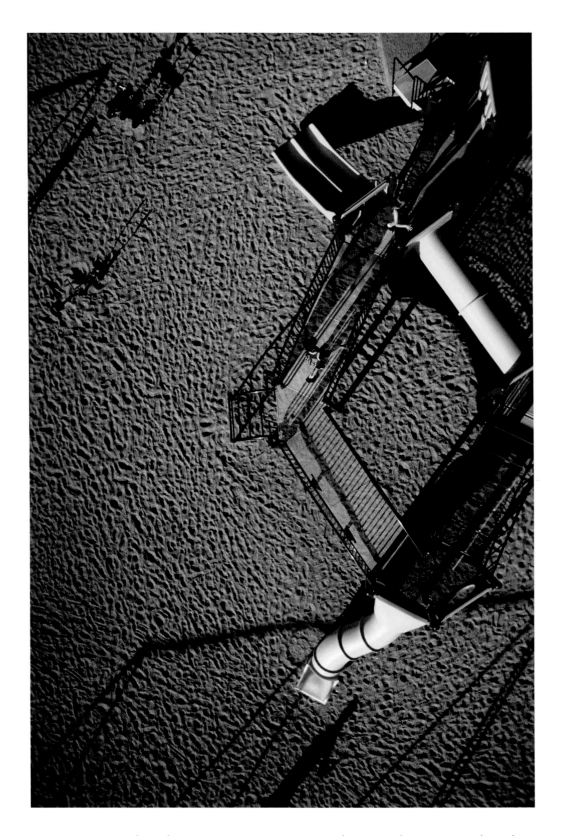

Continuous motion, Vilas Park • *Movimiento continuo, Parque Vilas* • *Ständige Bewegung, Vilas Park* •
维拉斯公园，持续不断的运动

Swinging friend • *Amigo en el columpio* • *Schaukelndes Kind* • 打秋千的朋友

Vermont Lutheran Church, Dane County • *Iglesia Luterana Vermont, Condado de Dane* • *Lutherische Kirche Vermont, Dane County* • 达讷县，弗蒙特路德教教堂

"X" marks the spot • *La "X" marca el lugar* • *Mitten im „X"* • 以 "X" 为标志的地点

Race for the Cure • *"Carrera por la Cura"* • *Laufveranstaltung zugunsten der Brustkrebs-Hilfe* • 为了治疗而赛跑

Volleyball game • *Juego de voleibol* • *Volleyball-Spiel* • 排球比赛

Nine Holes • *Nueve hoyos* • *Neun Löcher* • 九个洞的高尔夫球场

(right) Flag Day • *(a la derecha) Día de la Bandera* • *(rechts) Fahnentag* • （右）国旗日

(pages 112—113) Summerfest, Milwaukee lakefront • *(páginas 112—113) Festival de Verano, al frente del lago en Milwaukee* •
(Seite 112—113) Summerfest, Milwaukee-Seeufer • （第112至113页）密尔沃基湖滨地带的夏日节

Basking • *Disfrutando del sol* • *Aalen in der Sonne* • 日光浴

Building as sculpture, Calatrava addition, Milwaukee Art Museum • *Un edificio como escultura, adición Calatrava, Museo de Arte de Milwaukee* • *Gebäude als Skulptur, Anbau von Calatrava, Milwaukee-Kunstmuseum* •
密尔沃基艺术博物馆里雕塑式的建筑：卡拉特拉瓦的延伸部分

a different point of view

       The Calatrava addition to the Milwaukee Art Museum strikes me as a building about to jump up and fly off. Santiago Calatrava's designs are so different, so surprising, that they challenge our perception of how buildings look. It is the perfect subject for my kite and camera.

       The first photos of Earth from space changed our perception of our world. The Hubble telescope gave us new views of our universe. Architecture, music, art, technology, and even fashions constantly change how we see things. We are always looking for new ways to see our place in the environment. That's why kids climb trees, why tall buildings have observation decks, why we want the window seat on the airplane, and why we love a Ferris wheel. My camera on a kite provides that fresh point of view, and is as natural as standing on tiptoes, to see just a little farther.

Shore Bird, Calatrava addition, Milwaukee Art Museum • *Shore Bird, adición Calatrava, Museo de Arte de Milwaukee* •
„Ufervogel", Anbau von Calatrava, Milwaukee-Kunstmuseum •
密尔沃基艺术博物馆里的卡拉特拉瓦的延伸部分 —— 湖滨之鸟

(above) Streamliners, Calatrava addition, Milwaukee Art Museum • (arriba) Streamliners, adición Calatrava, Museo de Arte de Milwaukee • (oben) Stromlinienformen, Anbau von Calatrava, Milwaukee-Kunstmuseum •

（上）密尔沃基艺术博物馆里展出的卡拉特拉瓦的延伸部分——流线型物体

(pages 118–119) Milwaukee skyline from Lake Michigan • (páginas 118–119) Perfil de Milwaukee desde el Lago Michigan •

(Seite 118–119) Skyline von Milwaukee. vom Michigan-See aus gesehen •

第118至119页）从密歇根湖到远处地平线的密尔沃基全貌

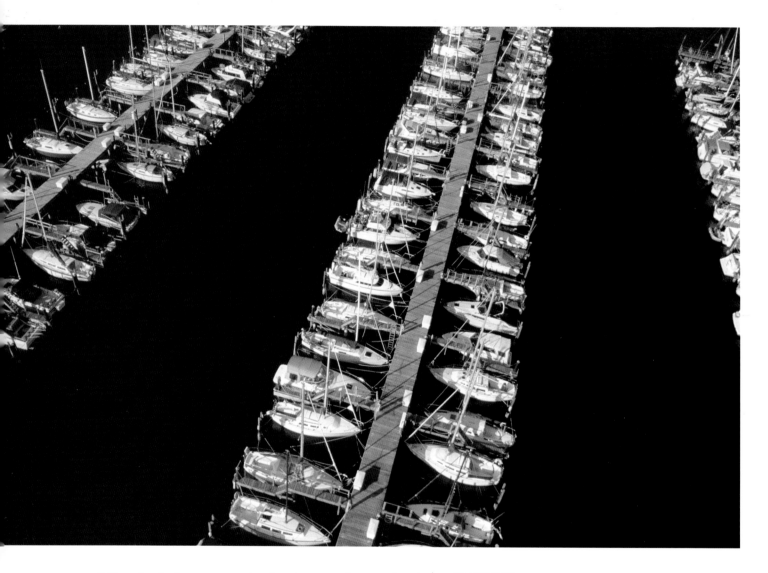

Milwaukee harbor • *Puerto de Milwaukee* • *Hafen von Milwaukee* • 密尔沃基港

In tents/Intense, annual AIDS ride • *En las carpas, evento anual en contra del SIDA* • *In Zelten: Auf der jährlichen
AIDS-Fahrt* • 年度爱滋病骑车比赛，在帐篷中/奋力向前

(left top) Milwaukee harbor • *(arriba a la izquierda) Puerto de Milwaukee* • *(links oben) Hafen von Milwaukee* •
（左上）密尔沃基港

(left bottom) Harley dudes • *(abajo a la izquierda) Fanáticos de Harley* • *(links unten) Harley-Fahrer* •
（左下）在哈利（Harley）的度假者们

(above) Harley party, Milwaukee waterfront • *(arriba) Fiesta de Harley, a las orillas de Milwaukee* • *(oben) Harley-Party,
Milwaukee-Ufer* • （上）密尔沃基湖滨地带，哈利聚会

Mitchell Park Horticultural Conservatory • *Conservatorio Horticultural Parque Mitchell* • *Gewächshäuser des Mitchell Park*
Horticultural Conservatory • 米切尔公园园艺温室

Mitchell Domes, Milwaukee • *Domos Mitchell, Milwaukee* • *Mitchell Domes, Milwaukee* • 密尔沃基，米切尔圆形建筑

(above) Sun Prairie Family Aquatic Center • *(arriba) Centro Acuático Familiar Sun Prairie* • *(oben) Freizeitbad Sun Prairie Family Aquatic Center* • （上）太阳牧场家庭水生物中心

(right) Sun Prairie water slide • *(a la derecha) Tobogán de agua en Sun Prairie* • *(rechts) Wasserrutschbahn, Sun Prairie* •
（右）太阳牧场滑水

Summers Christmas Tree Farm, Middleton • *Granja de Árboles Navideños Summers, Middleton* • *Summers Weihnachtsbaumfarm, Middleton* • 米德尔顿，夏季圣诞树农场

Kite tails over Wexford neighborhood, Madison • *La cola del papagayo encima del vecindario de Wexford, Madison* •

Drachenschwänze über dem Wexford-Stadtviertel, Madison • 麦迪逊，风筝的飘带飞过威克弗德街区上空

about the photographer

Craig Wilson has been a kite flyer and builder since 1983. He uses his large kites to lift radio-controlled camera equipment. He has flown his kites and camera system and exhibited his photographs in France, Germany, England, Japan, Belgium, Holland, South Africa, and in many locations in Canada and the United States. His images have been published in magazines and books, and used in advertising. Craig lives in Madison with his wife, two children, and dog, Stampy.

Craig is in ten photos. Did you find him? (Pages 1, 15, 31, 33, 86, 92, 97, 101, 107, and 130) • Craig aparece en diez fotos. ¿Lo consiguió? (Páginas 1, 15, 31, 33, 86, 92, 97, 101, 107 y 130) • Craig ist in zehn Photos zu sehen. Können Sie ihn finden? (Seite 1, 15, 31, 33, 86, 92, 97, 101, 107 und 130) •

10张照片上都有克雷格。你找到他了吗？（见第1、15、31、33、86、92、97、101、107以及130页）

A Giant Leap • *Un paso gigante* • *Ein Riesensprung* • 巨大的飞越